ABC's of Motorcycle Wrenching

Jasmine's Wrenching Tips

Published by Bluecreek Art Works
August 2009

Copyright © 2009 Bluecreek Art Works

All rights reserved. No part of this book may be reproduced in any form or by any means without the prior written consent of the Publisher and Author, excepting brief quotes or excerpts for the purpose of reviews.

Disclaimer: The decision whether to work on your motorcycle or not is a personal choice. It is possible to do serious damage to both your machine and yourself. Jasmine and Bluecreek Art Works and Motorcycle Training created this book to be an aid in understanding how your motorcycle works. It is not a substitute for professional repair work done by a certified mechanic or technician. In some cases, working on your own motorcycle could void your warranty, if your motorcycle is still under a manufacturer's warranty.

While the information in this book is true and complete to the best of our knowledge, motorcycle technology is a rapidly changing field. All recommendations are made without any guarantee on the part of the Author or Publisher, who also disclaim any liability incurred in connection with the use of the data or general or specific details included within this book.

We recognize that some words, model names and designations, motorcycle and tool manufacturers for example, mentioned herein are the property of the trademark holder. We use them for identification purposes only. This is not an official publication of any product, brand or model.

Printed in the United States of America First Printing August 2009

Cover Design, Layout, Text, Book Design: Jasmine Bluecreek Clark
Photography: Jasmine Bluecreek Clark and Roger Clark

Thanks to the Ladies from the mc maintenance classes for sharing their pictures and their motorcycles with all of us.

Bluecreek Art Works
Arvada, Colorado 80002
Contact information: www.bluecreekartworks.com

2nd Edition September 2009

ISBN 978 0 578 03504 8

Jasmine's Motorcycle Wrenching Tips

TABLE OF CONTENTS

CHAPTER 1
Tools & General Tips... Page 9
Hand me the *what?*
What Tools should I carry on my motorcycle?

CHAPTER 2
Pre Ride Check...Page 18

CHAPTER 3
Lights and Electrics...Page 22
Replacing turn signal bulbs and brake light bulbs
Replacing your headlight
Aiming the headlight

CHAPTER 4
Batteries...Page 27
Checking Connections
Checking the Charge
Can I check the fluid level?

CHAPTER 5
Filters...Page 31
Checking Filters, Why is this important?
Replacing or Cleaning the Air Filter

CHAPTER 6
Tires & Wheels...Page 34
Important Info... your life depends on these

CHAPTER 7
Checking your Cables...Page 38
Does my bike have cables?
Where the heck are they?
Lubricating the Cables

CHAPTER 8
Chain, Belt or Shaft Drive...Page 44
Which do I have?
Adjusting your Chain or Belt Drive

CHAPTER 9
Oil & Other Fluids...Page 50
Checking and/or Changing Fluids
Radiator Fluid

CHAPTER 10
Spark Plugs...Page 54
Checking &/or Changing
How to 'Read' the Spark Plugs

CHAPTER 11
Brakes...Page 60
Adjusting Drum Brakes
Checking Brake Fluid Level
How do I know if my brakes need bleeding?

CHAPTER 12
Motorcycle Ergonomics...Page 63
Can I make my motorcycle 'fit' better?
Easy Customizing for Beginners

CHAPTER 13
How to avoid sounding like an idiot at the shop...Page 69
How to talk to a Motorcycle Technician

About the Author ... *Page 76*

Tools 1

Hand Me the What...?

Tools are primarily metric or standard; metric tools always for foreign motorcycles and standard for American-made bikes. You will have to determine which type your motorcycle uses. Other tools, such as Torx wrenches – have their own sizing – neither metric nor standard.

Nothing is absolute – most American made mc's also use a few metric bolts these days and if another non-professional 'mechanic' has worked on the bike – all bets are off as to what size nuts and bolts may have been substituted in. Some American made bikes such as the HD's V-Rod and Buell models and Victory's Cruiser line mainly use metric bolts. You will be able to learn the difference.

Let us start with wrenches: there are so many different ones! You certainly won't need them all to work on one motorcycle. Eventually you will need to determine which tools fit and work on your bike and then don't worry about the rest.

Wrenches, in alphabetical order:

Allen-head wrenches includes sockets, t-handles, fold-em-outs singles and drivers

Box-end wrenches, Open-end wrenches and Combination Wrenches, these usually have one open end and one box end, but are available in all sorts of variations these days.

Crescent Wrenches: Adjustable wrenches in all sizes.

Oil Filter Wrench: various types available (see chapter 9)

Ratchet-head Wrench – common sizes include 3/8" drive, ¼" drive and ½" drive - drive meaning the size of the square peg on the end of the wrench where the sockets attach. You can attach metric or standard sockets to these ratchets.

Spanner Wrench for adjustable shock absorbers.

Torx Wrench- t-handles, sockets, singles, fold-em-outs and drive

I'm a firm believer that a Picture is worth a 1,000 words so let's look at some...

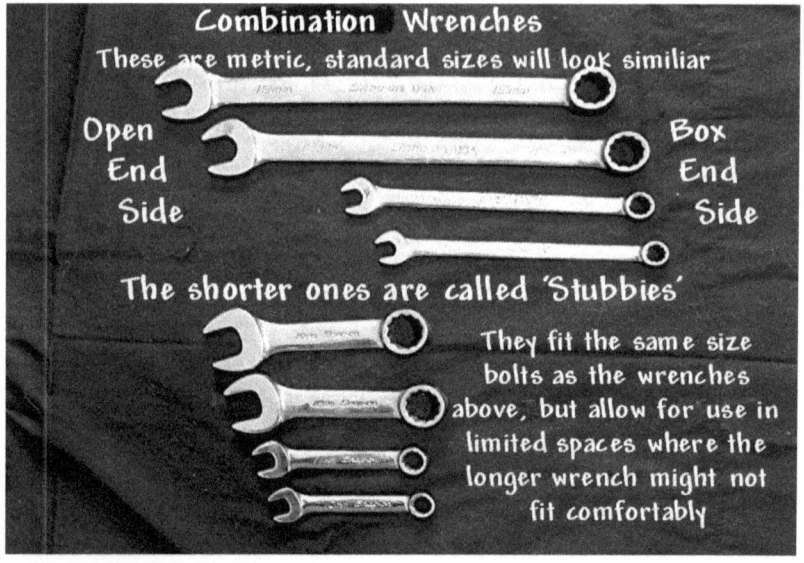

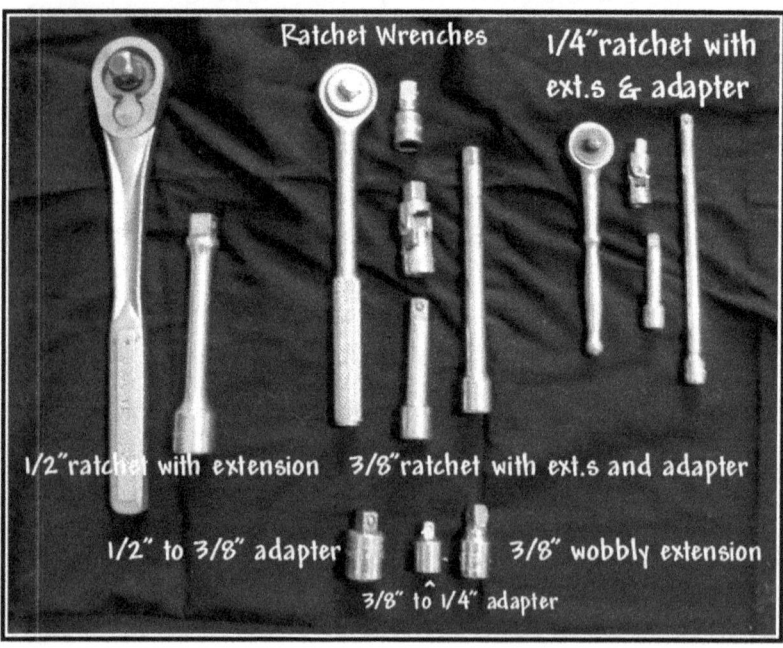

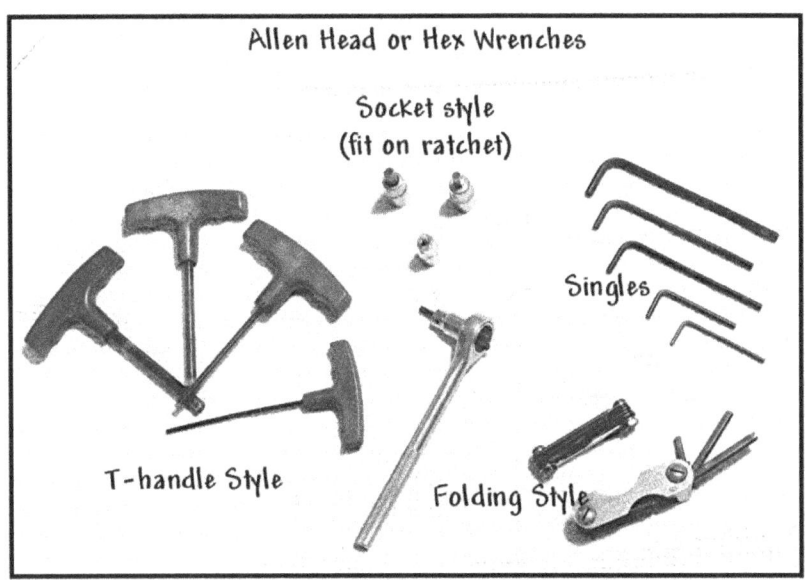

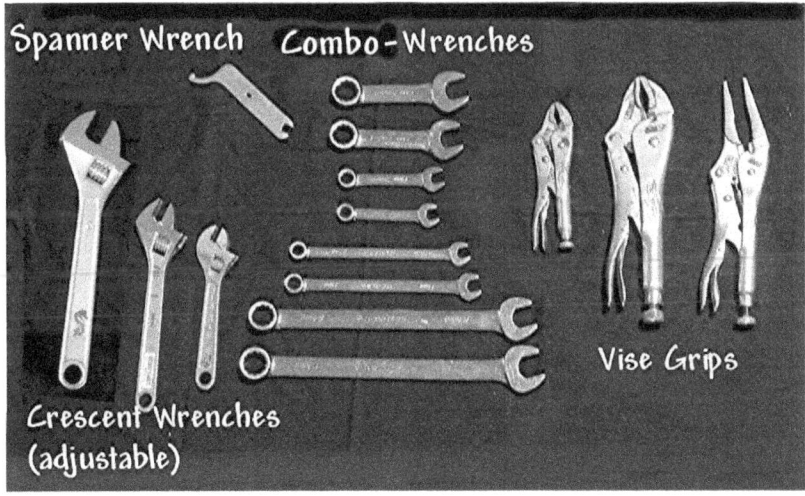

Other common Tools you'll want to be familiar with include:
Screwdrivers: Flathead and Phillips-head
Pliers: Needle-nose, right-angle, regular
Vice Grips: adjustable, locking pliers
Spark Plug Tools: see chapter 9

~~* *Your Notes* *~*~*

My Motorcycle Uses – Which Wrenches?

◇ **Allen Head Wrenches**

◇ **Box End – Combination Wrenches**

◇ **Crescent Wrenches**

◇ **Torx or Tamper Proof Torx**

◇ **Spanner Wrench**

◇ **Others**

◇ **Metric**   ◇ **Standard**   or ◇ **Both**

Metric Tools that fit my mc

Standard Tools that fit my mc

Which Tools should I carry on the mc?

It's not all that hard to figure out. You simply have to get to know your mc better. Get out your trusty owners' or service manual. There is always good information in there about simple tasks such as oil, spark plug and battery changes. The pictures can help you locate the parts your trying to find and may also tell you the size of wrench you're going to need to remove or replace that part. Once you locate the part you plan to wrench on – try out the size and style of wrenches and other tools that will fit your bike. Many foreign motorcycles come from the factory with a small tool kit included.

Here's a thought. Let's say you or someone you're riding with has a breakdown out in nowhere land; maybe you feel unsure about using those tools yourself. Having the appropriate tools when a good Samaritan stops to help you out could make the difference of riding home or having to haul it back.

You'll want to have some kind of light available. This used to be a flashlight, but there are lots of options these days. Everything from ball caps with LED lights in the brim that shine straight out in front of you to those bicycle lights you wear on your forehead and other variations. Recently, I've been using one of those. They are great as wherever I turned my head to look the light is right there with me, and both hands free to work. Because they are on an elastic strap and smaller than a regular flashlight, I believe these kinds of lights pack better on the bike too.

I will give my minimal list of tools that I would travel with. I usually take more on a longer trip. Only you can determine what is right for you to pack.

- 10mm Open end wrench (fits most battery cables at the post)
- Flashlight or Headlamp
- Spark Plug Socket &/or Wrench as appropriate to your ride
- Spare set of spark plugs – gapped and brushed with anti-seize, so they're ready to throw in (chapter 10).

- Leatherman™ Tool (replaces several small screwdrivers, pliers, etc.)
- Large Phillips head Screwdriver
- Large Flat head Screwdriver
- Allen head and Torx wrenches (for lighting fixtures, exhaust and other covers)
- 3/8" drive ratchet and sockets that fit your mc (peg bolts, fender bolts, gauges)
- ½ dz. Plastic Zip Ties
- 6" – 10" long heavy gauge piece of wire (can be used to jump your starter and other uses)
- 4" – 5" medium or light gauge electrical wire (can be used to check computer codes)
- Spare fuses or Circuit breaker, as appropriate to your electrical system
- Tire Repair Kit
- Clean Shop Rags

To keep it all together I like my Wolftrax™ canvas tool wrap or my Snap-On™ Tool Wrap. They come in various sizes and wrap up the tools nice, tight and waterproof. You will have to choose something suitable for your ride, as there are many good options out there for mc tool storage. The kind of tank bags that are made for sport bikes for instance, might not be suitable for a cruiser. The bags that work well on the cruiser probably wouldn't even fit onto a sport bike. You get the idea. Besides, most of us don't mind doing a bit of shopping now and then, especially when it's related to our bikes.

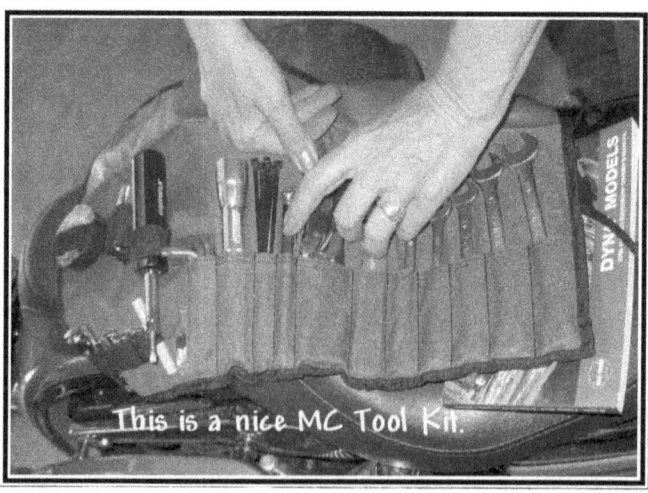
This is a nice MC Tool Kit.

General Wrenching Information and Tips

- Always check the simplest things first, don't immediately check for the worst case scenario – check the easy stuff first.

- Computer and Sensor problems will not be addressed in this book. It takes detailed electronic and computer training to diagnose and repair these sort of issues. While Jasmine has this training, it will not help you to try and deal with a computer or sensor problem if you have little or no specialized training in this area.

- Bolts come in all sizes, threaded and non-threaded. Threaded Bolts (the ones that need to be screwed in as opposed to tapped in) also have another significant difference.

Threaded Bolts come in 'coarse' threads or 'fine' threads styles. A 12mm coarse thread will not screw into a 12 mm fine thread opening and vice versa. A ½" fine threaded bolt will not properly screw into a ½" coarse threaded opening, etc.

- Never force a bolt, spark plug, or screw into an opening on your motorcycle. If it does not go in easily – there is something wrong. DO NOT FORCE THEM. FIND OUT WHY IT WON'T GO IN EASILY. Retry until they go in easily.

- Remove bracelets, rings, dangling earrings, hoop earrings, etc. before attempting any wrenching

- Look at the big picture – the whole motorcycle. Look at the details – all the different parts. Look again at the big picture. Look again at the details. Look again and SEE what you are looking at – before you ever pick up a wrench to touch your beloved bike.

- Be sure to read ALL DIRECTIONS BEFORE you attempt any new wrenching project. This includes your owners or shop manual information as well as information from this book. If you are still unsure – ask someone who is familiar with the procedure before you start.

- Throughout this little book – your owner's manual will be referred to as 'MoM' for Motorcycle Owner's Manual.

- It often helps me – if I'm not sure what the part I'm looking for should look like – to get the new part and have a good look at it. Then go and find that same part on your motorcycle. Of course, your MoM will tell you the general area of the bike to look for any given part.

- Loc-tite™ is a great product when used properly. Be wary of using Loc-Tite™ or a similar product on any part of your motorcycle. There are very few circumstances when using Loc-Tite™ on a mc would be recommended. If you are hell-bent on using some – never use the red or permanent stuff. Use the blue Loc-tite™ which is somewhat removable.

Traveling Tips – Road Trips

- Always pack so your most valuable possession – for us ladies that would usually be our purse or fanny pack (the bag that holds your ID, money, cell phone, insurance and towing papers) – Always pack this on top or somewhere with easy grab and go access. This makes stops easier, as you can carry your valuables into service stations or convenience stores as needed without disturbing everything in your saddlebags every stop. I also pack my camera in this same way – top, easy access. When out riding, you never know when you'll have a 'Kodak Moment' and want the camera

- Any time you see or smell smoke, flames or hear a high whiney whistling sound - shut the mc down immediately, especially the fuel valve if applicable. Grab your keys and your hand bag (if it's handy) and move quickly as far away from your mc as you can. Something could be about to blow up. *RUN AWAY! Not out of sight – but run FAR!*

- If your motorcycle needs attention roadside, be sure to ride or push it as far off the road, away from the traffic as possible first. This frequently means pushing it into a gravel or dirt shoulder. Avoid stopping in a curve. Instead find a long straight-a-way. This will give curious traffic more notice that you are there.

- Work on the bike facing and body turned towards the roadway. Always keep one eye on the roadway and all traffic. This way, hopefully, you will see a wayward driver before they collide with you or your motorcycle, giving time to jump out of the way if necessary. Riders do get killed every day along the side of the road.

- Use caution as to where you put down the kickstand. A smooth rock or flattened soda can will work as a side stand puck if necessary.

- If you need to work on the motorcycle roadside – it will likely be very hot. Keep your mc gloves on or wrap your hands with something before reaching in near the engine, brakes or exhaust. Everything will be HOT. Even Better... take a longer break and let the machine cool off a bit first.

- Remember to always Ride your own Ride – keeping up with the other guys isn't always the best goal. Live to Ride and Ride to Live.

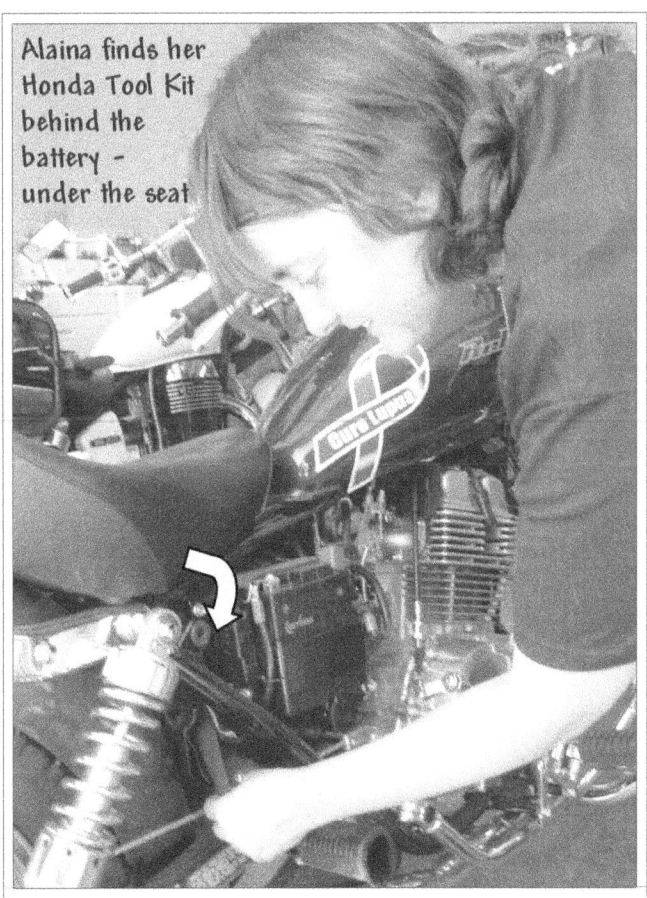

Alaina finds her Honda Tool Kit behind the battery - under the seat

Pre-Ride Check   2

Are you tired of reading yet? How about we go out to your motorcycle and have our first hands-on lesson?

Here the full list of the things to check out before every ride:

- **Tires and Wheels**
- **Electrics**
- **Fluids**
- **Controls**
- **Drive System**
- **Stands**

If you only check one thing on your motorcycle – it should be your tires – so we'll start there.

Tires and Wheels There are several things to check. Air Pressure is important – if you have the stock tires from the manufacturer on your motorcycle, you can read your owner's manual (MoM) to learn what the proper air pressure should be. Air Pressure is measured in PSI or Pounds per Square Inch. You will learn that you can vary your air pressure depending upon how much weight you are carrying on the bike. The owner's manual is the place to read about the different air pressures you would want when riding solo, with a passenger, or when loaded down to head out of town.

Other things you should check include tread depth, sidewalls, wheel rims and spokes, if you have them. Please read Chapter 6 for in-depth explanation of tire maintenance.

Electrics Just before a ride you should turn on all your lights, turn signals, horn, etc. and make sure they are working. Be sure to turn the key on first! Applying either brake should activate the brake lights – are they both working?

It's that simple. If you find any burned out bulbs – see Chapter 3 for information on how to replace them.

Fluids Well personally, I hate to be the one that runs out of gas or oil on a group ride. Do yourself and your riding buddies a favor and check all the fluids before you head out. Of course you'll want to check the gas, oil, coolant, etc. for condition and proper fills. The owners' or shop manual will give you all the specs you need for these jobs. There is more information on checking and changing fluids in Chapter 9. If you've seen any fluid under the bike since it's been parked, find out what, where it's coming from and why.

Controls This is one of the easiest checks of all. Just roll the throttle on and off – is it smooth – free of any catches or snags? What about the brakes? Does the lever and pedal work smoothly without noise, grinding or sticking? Same with the clutch lever – just use it as normal. Does it move smoothly in and out?

You will also want to look for frayed wires at the handgrips – Chapter 7 gives more details on how to do this.

Drive System This isn't difficult either - first you need to identify whether you have a belt-drive, chain drive or shaft drive system. Just look back there at the rear wheel. Is there a chain attached to it, a belt, or an enclosed shaft? Once you've determined what you have - go to Chapter 8 to read how to check and or adjust these things.

Side or Center Stands Most motorcycles have either a side stand, commonly called the kick stand, or they have a center stand. Some vehicles have both. Generally speaking you will just want to make sure that it works. Can you freely kick it into place or does it hang up or stick at some point. A little WD-40™ or similar lubricant will usually fix a sticky kick stand.

If it seems unusually loose, get down on your knees and have a look at the mounting hardware. First of all make sure all the bolts and nuts are there, (sometimes they rattle loose and fall off). Assuming they are all there – make sure the bolts and nuts are all fastened tight. You will want to take the bike off the stand to tighten them. If you have some sort of home lift - use that or have a friend or lover straddle the motorcycle to hold it upright while you tighten the kickstand bolts.

On the very rare occasion, I have seen welds (where two metal pieces come together) develop cracks or even break loose from the frame on stands. Have a look out for this condition if your motorcycle seems to be leaning over farther and farther, or the stand feels loose.

Ok, that's it. Not so bad huh? A pre-ride check should not take more than a few minutes to complete and you will get faster at it as you become more familiar with your motorcycle. This is also a good way to get more familiar with your ride and to notice new problems that might be developing before they become serious. *Have some fun getting to know your bike better!*

Check Your Tire Air Pressure Often
~ It's Easy ~

~~* *Your Notes* *~*~*

My Front Tire should have _____ **PSI**

My Rear Tire should have _____ **PSI**

Tires and Wheels - Last Checked On:

Date:
Notes:

Lights and Electrics – Last Checked On:

Date:
Notes:

Fluids – Last Checked On:

Date:
Notes:

Other Checks Performed:

Lights and Electrics 3

 Replacing Turn signal bulbs and Brake light bulbs

While teaching my mc maintenance class, I've met a couple of turn signal bulbs that were difficult to replace. In general though, this is one of the easiest things for a rider to learn to do. A lot of the orange lens covers simply pop off. You can use a very small flat head screw-driver (#1 size) to gently pry them off.

Pry a little on one side and if it doesn't pop right off, then alternate sides, prying a little at a time so as not to break the plastic covers. The ones that don't pop off usually have one or two small Phillips head screws holding them in place. Remove the two screws to access the bulb on this type. The Lens Covers for the brake lights are removed in similar fashion.

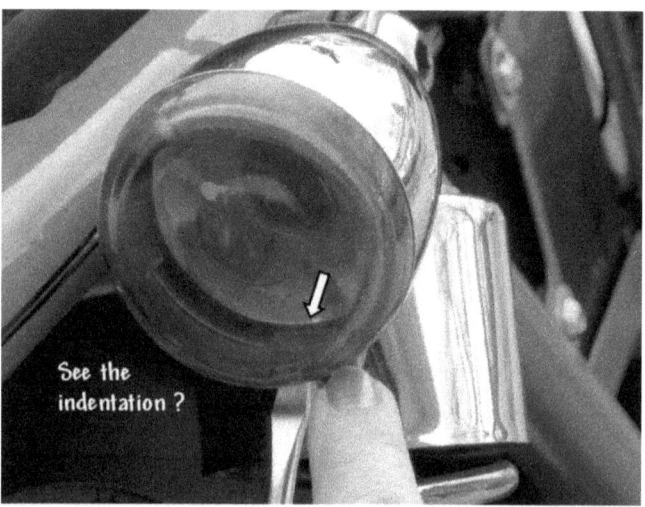

See the indentation ?

The bulbs themselves may seem mysteriously stuck in the socket, but it's actually really simple to understand.

You push the bulb in just slightly and then give a gentle little twist. If it doesn't want to turn in the direction you first try, simply press in again and try the other direction. At this point, the bulb will pull straight out.

To install the new bulb reverse the process, That is: Gently slide the bulb into the socket. Press it a bit more. A small twist will slide it right into place.

Important Points to Remember:

- Be sure to use the same # and size of bulb. Some have one electrode, some have two – you don't want to mix them up. There's some tiny numbers on the light bulb, 1056 or 1157, whatever... you want to match those up.

- As you remove the burned out bulb – take note of the little bumps or nodes on the sides of the light bulb. These two are placed at differing heights along the side of the base piece and must be re-inserted in the same direction as they come out. If you look into the socket with a flashlight you will see the perpendicular grooves that these nodes fit into. This helps you visualize the correct direction to reinstall the new bulb.

- Note that Halogen bulbs must not be touched by your hands as the natural oils will ruin the light. We install these by holding them with a rag.

Replacing your Headlight

Have you ever wondered if your light is shining in the right place? Is the light getting dim, or burned out totally? Have you wished your headlight was aimed just a bit higher or lower? If you ever dropped your bike, maybe the headlight doesn't even shine straight ahead anymore? I know at least once, on my old '84 Harley Roadster, the headlight was knocked sideways and shone about 6 feet up in the air and off to the right quite a ways. It can really suck if the light is not where it should be – in front of you – illuminating the roadway, especially if you're out riding after dark.

You may be surprised to find out that it is pretty easy to check, change and/or aim the headlight. The following directions are fairly generic, you should always check with your MoM first – in case your bike has a different set up for adjusting the headlamp than described herein.

Replacing the headlight should be pretty easy. Look to see what is holding it in place – usually a chrome ring commonly called a 'beauty ring'. These are generally held on with a simple clamp that has only one little screw. Loosen this enough to gently pull your headlight from the socket and through the beauty ring. On some motorcycles you'll remove the beauty ring completely first. Remember to keep track of where you set the tiny screw that holds it together.

The headlight is plugged in right behind the light and sometimes needs just a bit of GENTLE wiggling side to side to break it loose without breaking the light or socket. Be sure to replace with the same exact bulb unless you are upgrading to a better kind of light, for example a halogen bulb*. In that case make sure a trained tech gets you the correct one that will work on your model motorcycle. Then, just plug it back in, tighten the beauty ring and we're done!

Aiming the Headlight

To properly aim your headlight tape or draw a horizontal mark on a garage wall or screen that is the same height from the ground as the center of your headlight. Position your motorcycle on a level surface about 25 feet away from your test mark. Have a rider sit on the bike to simulate actual running conditions. The motorcycle must be upright with the front wheel pointing straight ahead. Turn on the key and then the high beam. The top of the main beam of light should be even with, but no higher than your horizontal mark.

If adjustments are necessary, loosen the headlamp mounting hardware and position the lamp to correctly adjust the beam. At the same time, move the lamp slightly to the right or left to direct the light straight ahead. Headlights enclosed in a faring may have screw adjusters built in, much like on an automobile, just under the clamp ring. Twist the screws a little in either direction to aim the light. After making all adjustments, tighten the mounting hardware, being careful not to change the adjustment while you're tightening the little screws back in place. You're all done!
It's just that easy.

The lens cap will pop right off on some models. No screws to mess with!

light bulb

~~*
Your Notes
~~*

My Turn Signal Bulbs are _____
                                                Light Bulb Number

My Brake Light Bulb is _____
                                                Light Bulb Number

My Headlight Notes:

Batteries 4

If you do not understand the information on these two pages — *Do Not* work on your own battery. Take the motorcycle to a shop.

For electrical problems, especially intermittent ones, first always check the easy stuff first: check the battery cables to ensure they are securely tightened to the battery. Then check your fuses and/or circuit breakers. If those are OK - then move on to checking for more complicated gremlins that can plague your bikes electrical systems!

Your owner's manual will show you where the fuses or circuit breakers are. They are either good or bad. Use a test light or volt meter to check if they are conducting current or not.

This is done by touching the grounded test light to either side of the fuse while turning the key or suspected part on. If the test light - lights up, the fuse and the circuits to it from the part you are testing are good.

If your mc battery is maintenance free, and most of them are these days, the only check is to make sure that it is charged and the cables are fastened tightly to the battery posts.

If you have the old style battery-with little colored caps on top* you also need to check the fluid level and top it off with *distilled water only* as needed. There are easily read marks along the sides of these batteries and you can see how much to fill it.

Caution: Batteries are filled with Acid; Never ever get any on your skin, motorcycle or anything else that you cherish. Always set the battery carefully on a work bench before you open any caps. Always wear gloves, safety goggles and protective clothing as necessary.

Checking the battery cables has to be one of the easiest things to do on your motorcycle. Locate the battery — if the location is not obvious, check your MoM to find out where it is hidden. Then simply grab onto one cable at a time and see if the wiggle or jiggle at the posts. They shouldn't move about at all. If they do — you'll probably need an 8 or 10 mm wrench to tighten them. Snug them down tight. That's all there is to it.

Never grab both posts at the same time. Never connect anything from the positive post to the frame or to anything else, except the positive battery cable.

Arcing:
Be careful not to touch the wrench or any other metallic object (bracelets, dangling earrings, metal flashlight - whatever) across both posts at the same time. This causes Arcing, as in the electrical current is jumping (arc – ing) across the terminals. NOT A GOOD THING.

Dropping something metallic on the posts will result in a lot of sparks flying around and could melt down your battery and your bracelets or other metal. You could burn your skin. Absolute worst case scenario, if you allow metal to arc across your battery and it is run by a computer – you could fry the computer brain as well as all the wiring throughout the motorcycle. Talk about your costly repairs – a computer and/or wiring - will be very expensive to replace.

This is easily avoided by being careful and maybe laying some non-conductive material (clean shop rag, bandana, mc glove or a small piece of wood) over the battery post side that you are not tightening. Then if you were to drop your wrench, it shouldn't be able to hit both posts at once.

Using a Volt Meter:
If your battery doesn't seem to be doing its job, i.e. the mc won't start or run its electrical components properly, a simple volt meter can be used to determine the following:

1) If your battery has any voltage in it at all.
2) If it is charging while the motorcycle is running
3) Whether the battery is holding the charge or not.

Set the meter for the 20 volt range and then touch or clip to both posts. With the motorcycle off, it should show 12 to 12.89 volts if it's fully charged. When the bike is idling you can do the same check. Rev up the motor a couple of times, now the meter should read 13v-14v on average. If so, this indicates that your charging system is working fine for the moment.

To 'Load-Test' the battery, have the meter connected to the battery while the bike is off and then watch it carefully as you try to crank or start the motor. Do this with the lights on. It will probably drop down to about 9 volts for a split second or two. It should recover back into the 12-14 volt range as soon as the bike starts up. If it dips below 9 volts and bike will not start – this means the battery is dead or dying and you need to charge it up or replace it.

If your bike has been parked for awhile you should use a battery tender for a couple of days prior to starting the bike for the first time. A one amp trickle charger could be used to charge it up also. These cannot be left unattended like the battery tenders. You will need to check them every couple of hours and turn down or off as the battery regains its charge. If the battery will not take a charge – you need a new battery.

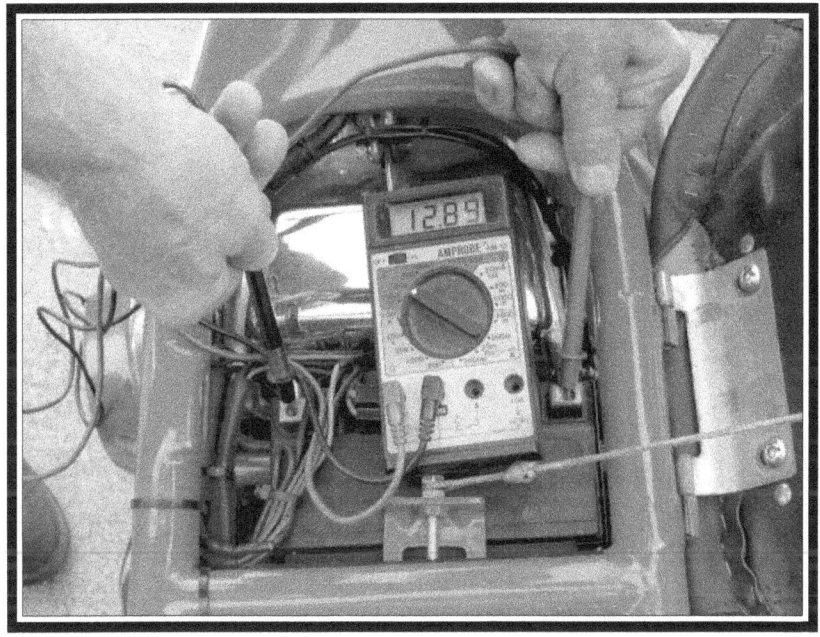

On this Harley Davidson FXR, the Battery is located under the seat

Replacing the battery will give you current again, but if the battery shorted out because your voltage regulator or some other part is really the culprit – your new battery will fail soon also. It's a good idea to have a competent mechanic check the bike's electrical system if you have recurring problems with the battery itself.

*Older motorcycles and off-road, dual sport and perhaps a few other styles may still use these old style batteries with the removable caps.

Filters   5

FILTERS: You don't really want or need to wait until they are shot to replace them. Replacing them routinely can increase the life and the output of your motor.

The filters on any engine are there to keep pollutants and other garbage out of your motor. Most mc's have an oil filter and an air filter, some have fuel filters also. Change the oil filter every time you change the oil. Whether it's a fuel, oil or air filter – be wary of aftermarket products. When it comes to filters, you should follow your manufacturers' recommendations to get the best results.

Check the air filter- it's really dirty if you cannot see through it when you hold it up to the light. It's time to replace or clean it. Some mc air filters can be washed out with dish soap and water. Some can be 'blown' out with an air hose. K&N™ sells a special cleaning kit for K&N™ filters. Other brands require replacing every time they are dirty. Some air filters are well hidden underneath the seat or gas tank. Others are readily seen on the outside of the engine. Read your owner's manual.

Some mc's also have fuel filters and these should be replaced as well. Not always easy to get at or find... you probably should let a trained mechanic do this job. However, if you really want to do it yourself – it is a simple job on SOME motorcycles and quite complicated on others.

Check your MoM – if the fuel filter is located in-line, under the petcock or in the fuel line to the carburetor – chances are you could change it out yourself. Frequently on late model fuel-injected motorcycles the fuel filters are inside the gas tank with the fuel pump. I would not recommend you trying to remove and replace this yourself.

If you decide you are up to the job - be prepared to catch all the gas that will probably spill out. Why not ride it till it is almost out of gas before changing the fuel filter? That way you get to have a fun day riding and you will have less gas to deal with.

You should certainly think twice before tackling this job solo the first time. Otherwise ask your regular mechanic to change the fuel filter per your manufacturers' recommendations.

Always be cautious around fluids and fuel in particular – no smoking – no cell phones – no open heaters – nothing that can spark, friction or flame anywhere near your work area.

Either use common sense with this one or take it to a real mechanic!

My Motorcycle has the following Filters

◊ **Oil Filter** _____
               Oil Filter Brand and Number

◊ **Fuel Filter**

◊ **Air Filter** _____
               Air Filter Brand and Style

◊ **Other Filters**

Checking the Air Filter by looking for sunlight to show through it

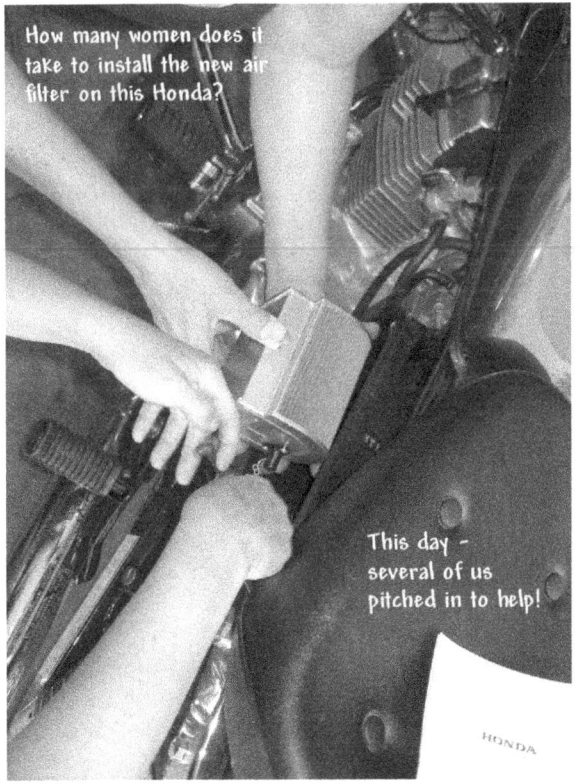

How many women does it take to install the new air filter on this Honda?

This day - several of us pitched in to help!

Tires & Wheels   6

What is the most common cause of tire failure? Think Hard: I can see your brow's furrowing now – Under-inflation! Running with too little air pressure is not only bad for the tires, it can make handling the mc tough. If you only check one thing on your motorcycle before riding – it should be your tires.

Around town, I check them at least once a week. When traveling cross country – I check the tires every morning. The only thing worse than having a tire go bad around town is to have it give out on you 200 miles from anywhere!

Riders often bring their bikes into the shop declaring a problem with the front end. Frequently the only thing wrong is the tire pressure is just way low. Cornering may feel 'mushy' or 'soft'. Now you're paying a mc mechanic $75 an hour to air up your tires for you! *Cute and expensive!*

The psi rating is written on the sidewall of the tires. You always want to check this when the tires are cold - before a ride. If yours' is a new mc with the stock tires still on it – your MoM will tell you the proper psi. The manual will give information on how much pressure to fill to when riding solo and with a passenger or load. Once you've put aftermarket tires on the bike you'll want to follow the recommendation on the sidewall. On some models the front and rear tires may not call for the same air pressure. Again check your owner's manual or the psi written on the sidewalls.

You can also email or phone the tire manufacturers. They want you to be as safe as possible while riding around on their product i.e. your mc tires. I've heard they are downright friendly and thorough in answering any and all questions you may have about proper tires for your riding style, type of motorcycle, correct psi, etc.

Other things you should check for regularly include looking for nails or other foreign objects in the tread which could lead to a flat or blowout and checking the rims and sidewalls. Simply roll the motorcycle at least one full revolution of the wheel and look for anything imbedded in your tires. Never patch a worn or punctured tire - GET A NEW ONE!!!! No reliable shop or mechanic will patch a mc tire for you. Only in the most extreme situations should you consider riding on a patched tire. If you must ride on a patched tire, plan to ride really slow to get to a safe place and be prepared to handle a blow-out if the patch should fail.

Check the sidewalls. Do you see lots of little nasty cracks or wrinkles? If you do, it's probably time to replace the tire no matter how much tread you have left. This is referred to as "weather checking" but sometimes it's called other names. It can be caused by too much exposure to the sun or other elements. Try to protect your tires from this by covering them when your bike is parked outside a lot.

Maybe your mc has been parked indoors for awhile and it still develops these cracks-what's up with that? Ozone, as emitted from electric motors can also cause this phenomenon. A freezer, an air compressor, or other electric appliances in the garage can contribute to the deterioration of your motorcycle tires.

The wheel rims should also be checked for dents, cracks or loose spokes. If you discover loose spokes – don't try to tighten them yourself. They need to be trued by a certified mechanic on a truing wheel. Have that done as soon as possible after discovering any loose ones. The longer you wait, the more dangerous your wheels are and also more spokes will rapidly loosen up.

Lastly, check the tread, 2/32nds depth is considered minimum by some tire experts, but that's awfully thin for my tastes. You will find there are wear bands/bars to help you see when the tire is getting too thin. Personally speaking, Roger and I replace our motorcycle tires way before they get that far down.

I suspect that the majority of injury-producing mc accidents - caused by defective equipment - are due to tire failure. Spend the five minutes or less that it actually takes to check these things; they will add up to a safer and smoother ride for you when riding time comes.

You can use a Lincoln's Head Penny to check your tread depth. When tires are new – his forehead is buried in the tread. As the tire wears down, more and more of Lincoln's forehead shows. If you can see all of Lincoln's head and hair when you stick the penny in your tire tread – it's about time for new rubber.

~~* *Your Notes* *~*~*

Front Tire _____ **PSI**

Rear Tire _____ **PSI**

Tread & Sidewall Check

Wheels and Rims Check

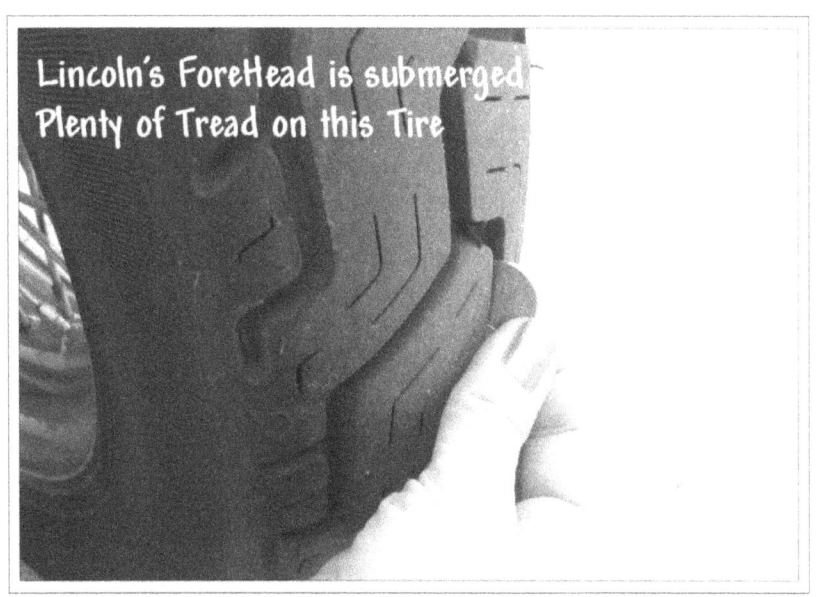

Cables 7

Does my bike have cables?

Well that depends... some motorcycles these days don't have any cables – or at least none that you can see. We're not concerned with internal cables because they may be hard to access and will probably require a professional's attention. Just figuring out how to get in to them is usually problematic in itself. Some Clutch Assemblies are hydraulic and don't use cables. Still some motorcycles have cables on them. Scarlett has Clutch and Throttle cables.

Where the heck are they?

The names give them away. Where would you expect to find a throttle cable? Attached to the throttle grip that you twist to accelerate maybe?

OK, you get three guesses where to find the clutch cable. Attached to the clutch side of the handlebars, near the clutch lever of course! Good for you!

Cables

Our throttle and clutch cables do need annual attention as in lubrication and should be checked regularly throughout the year for broken or frayed wires. Frayed wires are a sure sign that it's time to replace them asap. View the following pictures for how to check a clutch cable where it is most likely to break – where it attaches at the handgrip.

If your mc has a clutch cable, it's time to lubricate both that one and the throttle cable. Lubricating the throttle and clutch cables can prolong the life of the cable and prevent water build-up which can lead to rusting inside the sheath and subsequent unexpected breakage. It takes a bit of time for the oil or dri-slide to work itself through the entire length of the cable. For this reason I prefer to start lubricating the cables in the evening and let the lubricant have overnight to slip down the inside of the cable before I button it up to start riding again.

Janice is checking her Clutch Cable at the grips

Simply squeeze in the clutch and look up into the grip where the cable connects to the clutch lever. You are looking for broken or frayed wires. If you see any, have the clutch cable replaced.

Until recently, we always used cable lube which can be purchased at any motorcycle shop. These days, most techs prefer dri-slide™, a Moly Dry Film Lubricant. The dri-slide differs from the standard cable lube because it's dry and not oily but also the molecules are much smaller. This results in better lubrication and easier application. This stuff is also more toxic, so make sure to wear gloves and to wash your hands afterwards.

Whichever method you choose, at least once a year the cables need to be lubed. To ensure the best results and longest life of your cables I recommend twice a year – usually during the Spring and Fall. Read the directions on the lubricant container and see our pictures for help on how to lubricate the cables.

You will squirt in the oil or dri slide at the hand grips where the cables attach. You may have to open or remove your switch covers. This is easy enough. There are usually only 1 or 2 little screws holding these on. When you can see the end of the cable where it attaches near the handgrip – that is where you want to squirt the lubricant into the sheath.

As always, check your owners or shop manual for any extra information that might make accessing the cable ends easier. There may also be special recommendations for the proper kind of lubricant for your special motorcycle.

To Remove the Cover – First Remove the Screws or Little Bolts. They may be Phillips Head Screws, Allen Head Bolts, Torx head Screws – look at them closely to figure out which they are. These are being removed with a Phillips Screw Driver, how yours attach may vary.

Throttle Cables

After you lift the cover off – you should see the throttle cable(s) just under the cover. If you have two sides, a throttle and a return cable – both should be lubricated at the same time.

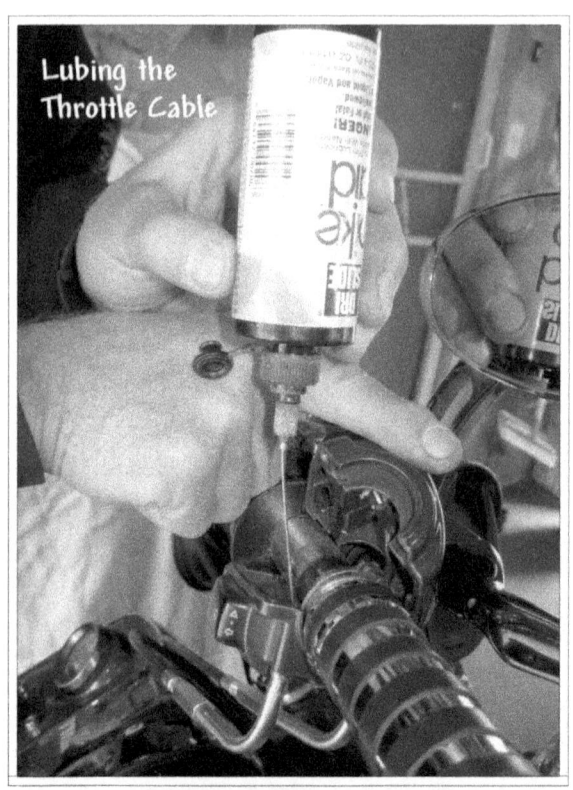

Does My Motorcycle Have Visible Cables?

◇ **Throttle Cables**

◇ **Clutch Cable**

~~*Your Notes*~*~*

Date Checked _____

Condition _____

_____

DRIVE SYSTEM 8

What kind of Drive System do I have?

It is a good idea to check your drive – belt, shaft or chain for signs of wear/leakage. Have a look back there at the rear wheel. Is there a chain attached to it, A belt, or an enclosed shaft? So far, these are still the 3 main types of drives on a motorcycle. Which is yours?

Chain Drive: If it's a chain, spray some chain lube on it before or after heading out. Lubricate that chain drive about every 400-500 miles year round. I recommend lubing it after a ride, this gives the oil time to settle into the links overnight and may not throw as much oil as when you apply it before a ride.

Shaft Drive: If it's shaft drive simply check it for leaks by running your hand underneath the shaft and case areas. Read the owners manual for times to change the shaft drive oil, but it is usually about every 40,000 miles or so. This is not a job most riders would have to do every year. But checking the shaft drive for leaks is a good idea.

Belt Drive: Belts should be looked over carefully and often. Sometimes you will see missing teeth – smooth spots where the rounded bumps on the belt have worn or broken off. If so, you need a new belt ASAP! Belts can develop weather-checking similar to the cracks found on the sidewalls of old tires; another indication it's time to replace it.

Belt and Chain drives should be checked for proper tension. Your owners' or shop manual can tell you how much play there should be (or not be) in the belt or chain and it's relatively simple to check. Most late model bikes actually have indicators at the ½ way point between the two sprockets that your belt or chain attach to, with measurements right on the chain or belt guard. This is where to check them.

For a chain drive, check how much play you have at the ½ way point. In other words, how far can you push that chain straight up? Around ¾ of an inch is a common range, but you must check with MoM for information specific to your bike.

Adjusting a Chain or Belt Drive

Chains or Belts that are either too tight or too loose can be easily adjusted at home. On many late model motorcycles you will find a 'cam' or 'gear' on the rear axle which can be easily turned either way to adjust the belt or chain tension. If you are fortunate to have this set up – you MoM can explain the whole process to you. These cams are already set up to turn both sides evenly. This takes the guess work out of it for you. It guarantees that you won't get your rear wheel cocked a bit off-center. Just remember to loosen the axle nut first.

On many motorcycles the adjustment is still manual. You will find the adjuster nuts behind the axle on the rear wheel, one on either side. There will be a slider for the adjuster bolt to move a bit forwards or backwards and two nuts. One is a lock nut and one is an adjuster nut. You will find this set up on both right and left sides of your back wheel. Some models do not have the lock nuts – so you will only find the one adjuster nut back there.

You should be able to twist the belt aprox. 90*
More than 90* - it's too loose
Less - it may be too tight

If you can twist your belt drive 90* at the half-way point it's adjusted about right. If it's too hard to twist, it's probably adjusted too tight. If it easily twists past 90*, it's probably too loose. This one is just right.

To Adjust Your Belt of Chain

Step 1 – Mark top dead center of the adjuster and lock nuts on both sides of the motorcycle with some fingernail polish or similar. Loosen the lock nuts on both sides, but do not turn the adjuster nut yet. Remember to mark both the right and left side nut exactly at the same top point. If they are too tight to easily break loose – use a spray lubricant like WD40™ or similar. Spray a little on and wait 5-10 minutes before trying again.

Step 2 – Loosen the axle nut – you will probably need a breaker bar or cheater pipe to help break loose the large axle nut. You may need to use an open-end wrench on the other side of the axle nut (other side of the wheel) to keep it from spinning. There is no need at all to completely remove the axle nut – just a few turns to loosen it will be fine. The Axle Nut is the big one that goes through the center of the wheel. Often there is a cotter pin which will have to be removed before you can loosen the axle nut. Replace it when you are done with a new cotter pin of the same size.

Step 3 – Determine which way you need to turn the nuts to:

a) Either loosen the chain or belt more – allowing more play in the tension
b) or To tighten up the belt or chain – less play or slap in it

In other words, if you need to tighten the belt and turning the adjuster nuts clockwise is the direction to tighten them – ONLY turn the adjuster nut on the left side ¼ turn. Then turn the adjuster nut on the right side ¼ turn.

I have often had to turn it a little in one direction or the other before I was sure which way is which. It's OK to play with it a bit – BUT – be sure to always turn both adjuster nuts EXACTLY the same amount in the same direction each time.

Step 4 - Straddle the bike – sit on the seat and bounce it a bit to help the adjustment settle in.

Step 5 - Re-check the tension at the mid-point between the two sprockets. If it is not where it should be – repeat steps 3-5 until you have the proper amount of play in the chain or belt. Remember – only turn the nuts ¼ turn at a time on both sides

– check it, then repeat as necessary. It doesn't take many ¼ turns to make a big difference in the tension so don't overdo it.

If your motorcycle had lock nuts behind the adjusters, now would be the time to re-tighten those. Be careful not to turn the adjuster nuts any more. Keep in mind that the chain or belt may tighten a bit more when you snug up the axle nut. See note next page.

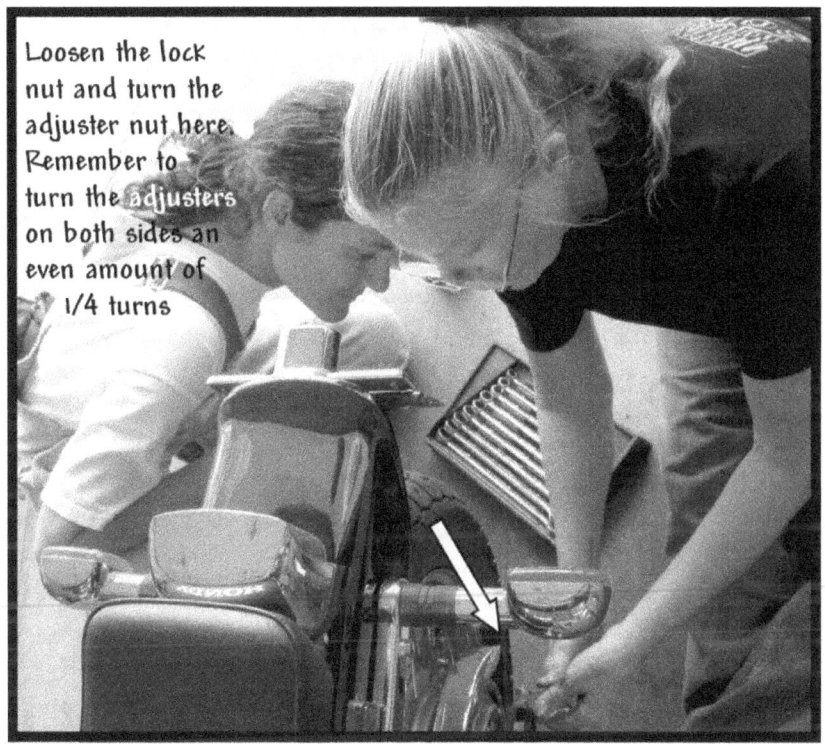

Loosen the lock nut and turn the adjuster nut here. Remember to turn the adjusters on both sides an even amount of ¼ turns

Turning the Adjuster Nuts the same amount of small turns on both sides is important

Step 6 – Retighten the Axle nut to the proper torque. If you don't know the proper torque – your MoM should be able to help. These days, you can probably look this stuff up on your manufacturers' web site also. Axle nuts – for obvious reasons need to be pretty tight. But proper torque for Luci's Honda Rebel may be a lot less ft. lbs. than the proper torque for my full size Harley FXR.

Note: With some motorcycles – you have to check the chain or belt drive tension with a rider sitting on the bike. Other motorcycles can be checked on the side stand without a rider's weight. Check with your MoM to be sure.

After Initial Adjustment sit on the bike and bounce the suspension a couple of times. Then recheck the chain or belt tension.

Luci bounces her Honda Rebel to help the adjustment she just made 'settle' before we check the chain tension again. Julie is watching the whole procedure.

Oil and Other Fluids

Levels: Of course it is important to keep all your required fluids filled to proper levels. All Internal Combustion Engines have at least gasoline and oil. Many also have transmission fluid, primary case oil and perhaps others. If your motorcycle is liquid cooled – you also have antifreeze – coolant - to deal with.

Condition: It is also important to ensure that the condition of the fluids is good. You do this by sight and smell. In other words, does the oil appear golden and clean looking or dark black? What is the consistency? Most fluids smell worse when they are old; they may smell burnt. They may look tainted or rusty.

Antifreeze: Is the antifreeze clean and sweet-smelling? If not, if you see brown or rust in there or it smells bad - you may want to replace the antifreeze. You will also want to check the freeze point in the Fall, to make sure you have a good balance of water and antifreeze. You need enough to get through the coldest temperatures in your area. An antifreeze tester is a simple tool that can be picked up at any auto parts store for a couple of dollars. Using it is practically self-explanatory. Just be sure to fill it all the way up for an accurate reading.

Transmission Fluid: What about the transmission fluid – what color and odor does it have? How much does your MoM tell you should be in there? What does MoM say about how to check the fluid level?

Fork Oil: I wouldn't recommend changing your own fork oil unless someone who knows how will be there to help the first time you try it. I tackled that one on my own the first time and when I loosened the second end cap the mc went bouncing over, springs went flying, it was quite scary. You should never loosen them both at the same time. That was the cause of that fiasco. The repair manuals don't tell you every little detail you're going to want to know - like that one. There was no permanent damage to me or my mc, so I lucked out, but serious things could've happened.

Engine Oil: It is of upmost importance that you regularly change your engine oil and the oil filter – your MoM will give you the manufacturers' recommendations for how

often. **We generally change ours more often than recommended, especially if it's right before a long trip.**

Engine Oil carries off all sorts of pollutants that can damage your engine. For this reason you don't want to wait too long to change the oil and you always want to change the oil filter at every oil change if applicable.

Some motorcycles have internal oil filters – in other words – oil filters that you cannot see on the outside of the engine, but some have an external filter, which you will be able to easily identify by studying with your MoM.

All engines will have an oil filler hole and a drain plug – you will have to identify these by use of the owners' or shop manual. Then simply open up the drain plug and drain out the old oil. It helps to have the cap off of the filler hole so that the oil can run out quicker. This will be a messy job, but well worth the effort as changing your own oil and filter can save you lots of money and is a fairly simple job on most motorcycles.

You won't want to scratch your motorcycle while removing the old oil filter and installing the new one. Those Strap style oil filter wrenches are really the best for motorcycles with nice paint jobs. They have a soft strap that is flexible; less metal to bump up against and scratch your fancy paint job or chrome.

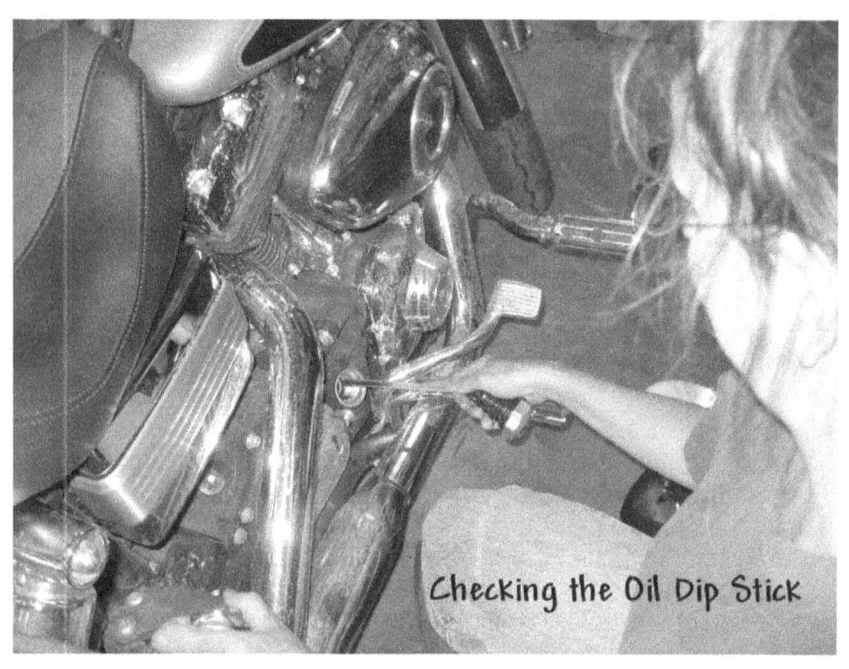
Checking the Oil Dip Stick

Refilling the Oil

~~*
Your Notes
~~*

Oil Filter _____
Oil Filter Brand and Number

My Motorcycle uses _____
How many Quarts or Liters of Oil

Favorite Brand of Oil _____

Oil Changes Performed

Date:

Date:

Date:

Date:

Date:

Spark Plugs   10

GOT SPARK?

If you don't, you probably aren't moving down the road too fast! Your motorcycle runs on spark plugs and if you forget to check, service or replace them every so often, you may someday find yourself on the side of the road crying *"The Bitch ain't got no spark!"* Don't blame your bike ~ *it's your job to keep her well tuned and purring.*

On many models, changing your own plugs is pretty simple. I've seen some brands that had hidden the spark plugs pretty well, making it difficult for the back-yard mechanic or novice to access them. On those types you have to remove much plastic (very-carefully) and in some cases, even the gas tank, to check or change plugs. It's worth considering taking it to the service department if so. I've also seen motorcycles from these same manufacturers whose spark plugs were easily accessible. On Harleys, most Honda's, some BMW's and many Suzuki's the spark plugs are visible and easily reached.

Whether you are the type who likes to wrench on your own ride, or you'd rather take it to your favorite mc technician - just make sure someone checks and changes your plugs according to the recommendations your MoM gives or anytime your mc is developing certain types of problems.

Fouled Plugs, Backfiring, Missing, Black Smoke, Sputtering, Power Loss, Stalling Out, Cranking, but not starting...

Oh I can hear you screaming *"STOP! STOP! WHAT'S WITH ALL THE FOUL LANGUAGE?"* These are all words/conditions Bikers and Riders dread to hear. Especially if someone is referring to your bike that is on the side of the road. All of these conditions can be related to fouled spark plugs. In some cases the condition of the engine will cause the problem and the spark plugs become fouled as a result of another mechanical issue.

Other times, the spark plug may foul out first, and be the actual cause of the problem. Fouling the plugs can happen from something as simple as you forgetting to turn off your choke soon enough (the number one fast way to ruin the plugs!).

Other times the carburetor needs to be adjusted. Any number of more serious engine problems can be discovered by 'reading' the condition of the spark plugs.

It is sure a relief to be able to get yourself and your mc right back on the road after a sudden problem. Many times throwing in a new set of plugs will clear out the engine enough to get you back to town and to your mechanic. If you don't have a spare set of plugs with you, you can clean the plugs you're riding with by scraping them with a small pen knife or fingernail file. You want to scrape off as much of the black carbon deposit on the electrodes as you can so that the spark can 'jump' across the gap again. This is not hard to do, but it can get rather messy.

- **Beware of Cross-Threading the Spark Plugs when replacing them. In other words — DO NOT FORCE the Spark Plug to screw back into the spark plug socket — if it doesn't go in easily by hand, back it out, reposition and try it again and again until it screws into place easily. Serious and Expensive Engine Damage can occur if you cross thread the spark plugs.**

- **Never use a big wrench to put the plugs back in — start them in ALWAYS, by hand. Use a wrench only to tighten them down after you are sure they are in there correctly**

- **Beware of OVER TIGHTENING your spark plugs — use the proper torque, as listed in your MoM. Proper torque is probably less tight than you expect it to be.**

- **IF THE BIKE IS HOT--SO ARE THOSE SPARK PLUGS! Use Caution when touching them while hot, or avoid touching them at all until the motorcycle has cooled off.**

If you are going to have to clean the plugs you are already using, I'd suggest planning on a nice rest where you are - till the bike cools off. BETTER is to always carry a spare set of plugs, already gapped to the correct measurement and already brushed with antiseize. This way they are ready to throw in with a minimum amount of tools aboard. Find the information on the spark plug gap and torque in your owners' or service manuals.

Always carry a spark plug wrench that fits your mc. Guess that means you're going to have to figure out what size plugs you have and what size and style of wrench will best work for your motorcycle. A lot of motorcycles include a small tool kit when you purchase them. These usually have a special tool or wrench of some type that fits your spark plugs. Learn which tool it is and how to use it.

Spark Plug Gap

Spark Plugs must be gapped (see photo). That means that the air space between the electrodes must be a certain measurement in order for your motorcycle engine to 'fire' properly. This is easily done.

First check in your MoM under 'specifications'. You should be able to find the recommended gap written in there.

For American made bikes it will be something like 0.038-0.042 inches; for metric bikes it will be something like 0.06 mm to 0.09 mm. A spark plug gapper tool will generally have metric numbers on one side and standard measurements on the other side - so one tool will work for either type. This same tool is very inexpensive and can also be used on spark plugs for your car, lawnmower, anything that has a spark plug.

You simply insert the opening in the spark plug onto the spark plug gapper. Slide it around until it is too tight to slide any further; no need to power-muscle this - a light touch will be more accurate. Be careful not to force the plug into a higher number than it is. Read where the plug stops at - and then figure out if that is the same, more or less than the recommended gap and adjust as necessary.

If what you read is less than the required gap - force the plug onto the gapper a bit further until you reach the desired number. Wiggling it gently back and forth as you are sliding it can help enlarge the gap.

Julie is carefully removing a Spark Plug using an open-end wrench while Janice looks on.

You would read this one as .045" spark plug gap

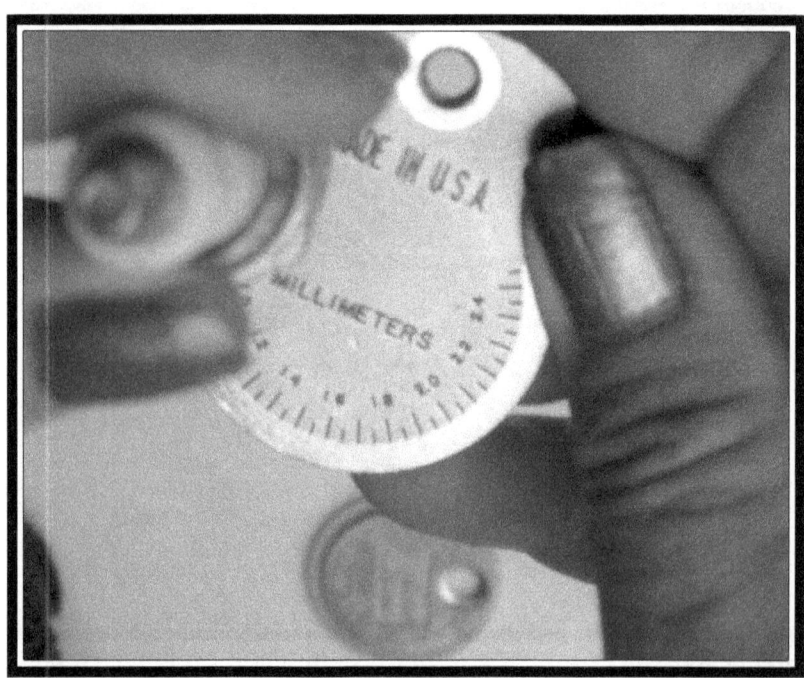

Reading Plugs

You can learn to 'read' your spark plugs. Heavy dry black deposits on your plugs means too much carbon, the bike is running too rich, too much fuel, too little air into the engine. Wet carbon deposits can also indicate a too rich air/fuel ratio, possibly caused by a restricted or dirty air filter (always check the easy stuff first). There are a half dozen other colors and signs to be read just by looking at the sparkplugs. These will give you and your mechanic clues as to how the engine is running and help diagnose internal problems.

Shop manuals often have this pictorial information on spark plugs as well. **If your motorcycle is running rough and you change your plugs - save the old plugs to show to your mechanic, it will help them diagnose the problem**. It's also helpful to mark which spark plug came from which cylinder - ie: front-back or left/right, etc.

Of course, all the new spark plugs in the world won't solve your problems if the mc's ignition wires (spark plug wires) are bad. The ignition wires need to be checked and replaced at regular intervals. I'd take a good look at them before any long trips. You are looking for cracks where the electricity could jump (arc) out.

For my Harley, I carry a regular 3/8" drive ratchet and the appropriate spark plug socket, a spare set of plugs, gapped and brushed with antiseize. I always gap my spare spark plugs before I leave on a road trip. Then if I need to replace my spark plugs while traveling I can carry one less tool on the motorcycle. I carry a couple of heavy rags in case I want to change them hot, I wrap my hands.

These things take up very little room, but could bring so much relief if ever needed. Then there's old Murphy! Murphy's Law says if you don't pack it with you - you'll need it, if you do pack it - you'll never need to use it. I prefer the second option for my road trips.

I am happy to say that *Scarlett Dancer* is much more reliable than previous bikes I have owned. Still I think I'll carry the extra plugs and wrench on my out-of-town rides. So keep the SPARK in your life and your *Ride.* Why not go out and check them right now? Spark Plugs are cheap and generally easy to change. Plus your mc will love you for it. **:)**

Brakes 11

Working on your own brakes carries a special kind of responsibility – don't you think? If you know what you are looking for, certainly check them yourself, but *if you are not sure what to look at - please have a professional check your brakes.*

Brake Lines How about brake lines, where would we find these? Yep, you're right – they will be traceable from your front and rear brakes back to their source – the master cylinders. Or you could go the other way round. Tracing the lines from the brake lever or pedal to the master cylinders and out to the brakes. The only check for these is to make sure they are not leaking fluid through anywhere. You can run your hand along the lines from the master cylinder to the brakes at the wheels. If they're dry, there is not much else to do. Since they carry brake fluid inside of them, we don't need to lubricate our brake lines.

Master Cylinders It's a good idea to eyeball those master cylinders occasionally and check that they are full of clean brake fluid. Make sure you get the correct kind of brake fluid for your machine. Dot 3 is commonly used in most cars and some motorcycles. Over the years Harley Davidson has used Dot 3, 4, or Dot 5, depending on the year and model. Read your owner's manual before topping off to ensure that you use the correct type of brake fluid.

Brake Pads You want to look at the brake pads and see that they have plenty of 'meat' on them. If you can't see the pads, they may be worn down and need replacing. Also check all the bolts on the calipers for tightness. If you find any loose bolts, leaking cables or leaks coming from either brake master cylinder (you should have two, one each for front and rear brakes) take it to a mechanic for appropriate repairs. Some Hondas and a few other makes still use drum brakes-usually on the rear only, but I still see some mc's with front and rear drum brakes. These need the pivot joint (located at the wheel) lubricated, usually with a moly-dry film lubricant product. Check with your MoM, or your local dealership to purchase the correct lubricant for the brake pivot joints aka: Actuating Arm.

Lastly, check for the adjustment. This is simply done by squeezing the brake lever/pedal and noticing if your brakes engage before the lever/pedal is all the way in/down. If you have to go to the max before you have brakes - most can be adjusted. If they have already been adjusted all the way out - it's time for new pads or shoes.

Do not skip, skimp, or put off replacing brake parts when you need them. Your life could depend on it and the repairs can quickly become more expensive.

Rhiannon (Jasmine's daughter) and Jasmine

If either brake feels 'spongy' or needs to be pumped before you can feel the stopping power – there may be air in the brake lines. This is a simple job, but if you don't know how to bleed the brakes properly – take it to a shop. You could actually introduce more air or even dirt into the lines if you do not know what you are doing.

Motorcycle Ergonomics   12

Does Your Bike Really Fit You?

I was wondering how many of you are happy with the 'fit' of your motorcycle. If you are not totally comfortable on your ride, some questions you might want to ask yourself include:

- Do your feet reach the ground well enough to easily balance the bike at stops?
- What about the width of the bike and of the seat, comfortable?
- Hands and Wrists – are yours comfortable?
- How is the reach to the handlebars and grips – comfy or stretched and strained?
- Do you like where and how your feet rest during rides?

If you answered no to any or all of those questions – you should know that it is not that difficult nor expensive to make minor changes that can add up to major improvements in comfort and handling.

Let's explore some of the different ways to customize your ride to fit you better.

Lowering Overall Seat Height

A lot of Suzuki GXSR's, DR's and others are designed with a mono-shock in the rear (yeah, I already knew that too). But I bet you didn't realize how adjustable they are. Victory Cruisers also have this adjustable mono-shock. While this isn't a job for an amateur mechanic (the entire rear suspension has to come off and back on) you can have this one shock adjusted to as much as 3" lower without buying any new parts. Suzuki technicians recommend not taking it down that far, but an inch or two is quite acceptable to help get your feet closer to the ground. The front shocks can also be lowered on many models.

A lot of cruisers use dual shocks in the rear. Often these can be replaced with shorter shocks to lower overall seat height.

Installing a new pair of shorter shock absorbers is generally a very easy job.

For Harleys you can buy a shorter front end or install a lowering kit. Another alternative is to install shorter springs – but only if you understand how this can change the handling of the bike. You would need to know how to maintain the suspension balance and that can be tricky.

Many American made motorcycles can be lowered by replacing or altering the seat. Shaving the seat on a Cruiser is a perfectly acceptable way to get a couple of inches nearer Mother Earth. Sometimes shaving the sides of the seat only, while retaining all the padding under the butt works well.

Sport bikes don't have a whole lot of seat to begin with. Dual Sport motorcycles can get seats 1" lower but that's it. The Sport Bike parts and accessories aftermarket is so huge, you can spend as much or as little as you want to make the Sport or Dual Sport motorcycle fit.

Hand Grips and Hand Operated Controls

How do your hands feel when you ride? If you like long distance road trips – even a comfortable fit can become numbing. If you have carpal tunnel or arthritis you may experience numbness or cramping pain in the hands or wrists. That's no way to ride, YIKES! How can we improve this problem?

Grips come in all diameters these days. Thick grips, skinny grips, hard or soft grips are all readily available at most any mc parts department. There are even some that are like big foam cushions. They make nostalgic grips and every sort of decorative design you could imagine. They can all be yours for a price. So there are no excuses for not alleviating those kinds of hand/wrist discomforts.

Now to the hand controls; can you easily reach your brake and clutch levers without removing your hands from the grips? We're talking safety here as in – if you can't quickly reach and operate that front brake and clutch – how are you going to stop quickly in an emergency situation?

I was really pleased to see that as of 2008, pretty much all of the Suzuki and Yamaha Sport bikes as well as the Victory motorcycles come stock with adjustable hand levers. You don't even need any tools. Anybody could adjust these. What a great concept. Although these levers have been around for a few years, they were not standard equipment until recently. You can't get much easier than this fix. For other brands of motorcycles you will need to remove and replace your levers. You can purchase a variety of lever styles which will bring the reach in closer for you.

Handlebar Height and Reach

Handlebar height and reach should be comfortable. When you're seated on the bike your elbows should be comfortably bent and relaxed, not stretched out to the maximum; certainly not crimped and cramped in too close. If you have to reach too far for the grips it can affect your overall control of the bike, especially in turns and corners.

Usually fixing this problem involves either changing out the handlebars and/or the risers. You will have to purchase new parts for this but the comfort and better control that results is worth the cost and effort. Many models of bikes can be equipped with aftermarket handlebars to better suit you.

Foot Placement

Lastly, what about your foot and leg comfort? Is that working for you? Can you easily operate the foot controls when you're seated on the mc? There are many options for foot positioning while riding. An obvious first choice is whether you will ride with foot pegs or floorboards.

All floorboards have height adjustments built into them. Adding a set of highway pegs on some models gives you another possible resting place for your feet and allows you to stretch your legs out on those longer rides. Sometimes you can have your foot pegs moved to a different spot on the frame.

Is the gearshift lever in a handy position for your foot? All Harleys and many other domestic and foreign brands have gear shift levers that are fully adjustable, making this another very easy fix that you could probably do for yourself.

I hope most of you are already comfy with what you ride. If not, it seems that the bottom line is that changing or modifying your ride as needed can be relatively inexpensive, fairly easy to do, will make the ride more fun and generally safer also.

~~* *Your Notes* *~*~*

Roger from Thunderbird Motorcycles with a group of women riders

Talking to Your Motorcycle Technician   13

There are many repairs that should not be attempted at home, especially if you are a novice mechanic. It's important to have a good relationship with your local dealership or after market repair shop.

This is another arena where women and men sometimes feel intimidated or inadequate. Even worse, you may have all the confidence and knowledge in the world but the staff may still treat you like an uninformed rider or (worse-case scenario) talks down to you. You should always remember that you are the consumer – you are paying them money to fix your mc, and if they are rude maybe you'd rather spend your hard-earned dollars somewhere else. I'd find another shop to deal with.

I've been known to walk out of auto and motorcycle shops when the guy at the counter starts feeding me a line of BS, or talking down to me because I'm female. Even so, how you present yourself and your motorcycle problem to the service writer or tech can go a long way in helping you to have a better experience at the shop.

First of all, why are you bringing the motorcycle into the shop? Other than routine maintenance it's usually one of these common things that will send you running to the mechanic:

1. **a No-Start usually gets your attention**
2. **an Unusual Noise**
3. **a Noticeable Handling Problem**
4. **Poor Running condition** (such as slow acceleration, missing - engine hiccups rather than running smooth, lack of power, backfiring, smoke & other symptoms).
5. **Brakes don't work well or make noise**

Believe me mechanics get "it doesn't start". What they need is just a small amount of information to be able to give you a reasonable diagnosis of the problem before they actually look at the bike.

#1: No Start: In what manner does it not start – when you turn the key – does anything at all happen? If not, make sure that the cut-off switch is also on, in the run position. If there's still nothing - that's all a mechanic needs to know to get started. If it makes some noise – is it cranking over & over, but not firing? Do you see the headlight dim as you try to crank the engine over? Does it fire, engage the engine and then quickly die out? Does it make a wheezing sound as it dies out?

What else can you see/hear/recognize that is different than a normal good start? A little information here will shorten up the time the mechanic needs to spend diagnosing the problem, create a bit of respect between you and the tech, and maybe save you some money on the hourly fees.

#2: Aahhh...Noises: I hear them all the time I'm riding some days. I'm just sure there is something about to break on my motorcycle because I think I'm hearing some weird noise or another. It's my imagination most of the time. Occasionally though – listening to the sound of my bike has helped me predict and prevent major issues by catching them early.

If you are hearing noises *and* your mc is not running or handling as it normally does – don't ignore them. First what kind of noise is it? Does it remind you of another sound you can use to talk with the mechanic?

Is it a high tea-kettle whistling, a ka-thunk a-thunk, a knock, squeak, rattle or wheeze? Can you see , hear or feel an air leak? Where is this sound coming from, between your legs - the engine? Lower than that – maybe in the transmission? Ahead or behind you a bit – is the sound coming from the wheels? Does the sound repeat with the wheel revolutions? You can test this by riding slow enough to hear the noise and speeding up to see if the sound speeds up also.

You should be able to give the technician a few clues as to when does the noise happen. Is it when you are accelerating or shifting? Maybe it's noisiest when you're at an idle or when you are decelerating? Again, improved communication with the tech and better knowledge of your motorcycle are our goals here.

#3: Handling Problem: If the steering or handling changes on your motorcycle from its norm... *HEADS UP*... this could indicate a number of serious problems – you should consider NOT RIDING IT until the cause is discovered. I have to say that 8 out of 10 bikes that come into my husbands' shop for handling issues simply need their tire pressure brought up to specs. So read Chapter 6 and learn how to check and maintain your tires.

Otherwise – if the air pressure in the tires is good – take a really good look at the front and rear wheels/spokes/wheel-bearings/brakes/shocks and tires. **If you cannot determine what the problem is – Don't Ride It! Call for a tow back to the mc shop.** Be prepared to tell the tech pertinent information such as what type of terrain you were riding when it started, ie: steep hills, curves or flatland. Was your riding speed slow or fast? Was it worse when leaning to the right or left side? What were the conditions when you noticed the problem? Were there any noises involved?

In these situations a mechanic really needs some additional information in order to readily discover what is wrong with your bike. Simply saying, "I don't like the way it feels" or "it just didn't feel right" won't help much. Trained technicians are just that – not mind readers. Undoubtedly, they will figure it out eventually, but the more time they have to spend diagnosing the problem, the more you are going to have to fork over for the repairs.

#4: Engine Issues: There is a myriad of problems that can fall into this category. Most of them are not for the amateur mechanic to tackle. **Any time your machine is losing mass quantities of any kind of fluid you must stop riding it immediately or serious engine damage *will* occur. It is quite possible to do serious damage to your lovely motorcycle while attempting to repair an engine problem if you are not qualified to do so. Basic maintenance is one thing – engine problems are a whole 'nother beast.**

We'll delineate some of the common symptoms now.

There are many reasons an engine might lose power, only a few will be addressed in the course of this book. Most would call for a certified mechanic to deal with properly. Your job is to be able to effectively describe the symptoms, so as to set your technician happily and quickly off in the right direction.

We don't need to know everything about our motorcycle engines to be able to intelligently describe the symptoms of the problem. Let's play 'Sherlock Holmes' with our machines. Look, listen and record any and all things different that you notice. Taking notes is a good idea. Remember to bring them with you as you head to the shop.

Think about it, when do you feel the lack of power? Is it when you are letting out the clutch? Do you feel it in all of the gears? Is the clutch slipping? Maybe you feel it most during acceleration, perhaps only in certain gears or only on up-shifts or only while downshifting.

Be prepared to describe the intensity; is it a slight loss of power when passing another vehicle or huge loss of power on take-off? Does it just sputter when idling and continue on, or sputter to a halt and shut down?

Is it smoking? If so, what color smoke do you see, gray, black, brown, blue? From what part of the bike? Is there a noticeable odor? Do you see any fluids leaking out? If so, record when, where, how much leakage or smoke and what color they are.

#5 Braking Issues: First of all, if you are hearing noises associated with braking – DON'T PUT OFF GOING TO THE SHOP and having it checked out. What if you can't stop when you need to because you ignored that scraping noise from the front wheel? Read Chapter 11.

If the pads are worn down – that is relatively inexpensive to repair, but if you continue to ride and brake – pretty soon you will destroy your rotors too. Now we're getting into some money.

Have you noticed that your pedal or lever is going all the way down/in? Do the brakes fade or grab as you apply them? Again, notice what is happening, so you can give educated clues and constructive information to speed along the repairs and communication.

Talking to the Tech

Try talking a friendly mechanic (male of female) into coming to your next riders' group meeting. Agree to hold the meeting in someone's garage with a competent teacher/mechanic and a real live motorcycle or two - to show ya'll a few things. You'll have a lot more confidence and be less likely to make any costly mistakes. Pick someone competent, as should be evidenced by their own fine running machines. *I'd avoid those backyard mechanics you might know whose bikes are always breaking down! Giggles!*

Lastly, when talking to your mc tech – don't try to tell them how to fix the problem or what parts need replacing. If you are already that smart you wouldn't be reading this particular book and you probably wouldn't even need to take your bike to a mechanic.

It often works better to *ask* the tech if he/she thinks it might be the so and so part rather than *telling* them what you think it is. They are the professionals - give them credit where it's due and let them do their jobs. Telling a tech how to do their job can create friction.

While I've met a few mechanics that don't mind their customers standing around while they work on their motorcycles - most don't like it. At best, you are in their way as they reach for tools. Worst case scenario – you are bugging them by hanging around and on many levels – you may be distracting the very person you are trusting to take good care of your machine – I would want my mechanic to stay focused on the problem at hand – wouldn't you? Could you work like that – with someone looking over your shoulder? A lot of technicians can't. They need to concentrate and focus to do a good job, just like the rest of us.

Generally speaking, if you treat the tech with respect you will get the same back and if you can help out by accurately describing the symptoms of the issue – you're on the road to creating a good will and an intelligent, lasting relationship with your motorcycle technician.

Motorcycle Maintenance Class, Summer 2008

About Jasmine Bluecreek Clark

You may wonder how a woman ended up learning so much about engines and wrenching.

Jasmine grew up in a very mechanical family with 3 brothers and her Father all being engineers and/or mechanics. Her Father was a Diesel Ship Engineer, trained by the US Navy. Later, he designed and manufactured improved parts for the old Fairbanks and Morse Marine engines.

Many days, when Jasmine was a child – she hung out at her dad's shop, growing up amid the smells and sounds of these large engines all around her. She remembers playing totally inside the clutch ring of the engines. She also remembers seeing grown men lying completely inside the engine block where the crankshaft belonged while they worked on the giant marine engines.

During the 1960's the whole family learned how to wrench on automobiles. Two of her brothers grew up and worked along side her dad in the marine engine shop, and one also became a motorcycle mechanic. Jasmine went on to earn her certificates in Automotive Technology in the early 1990's from Front Range Community College. She became ASE certified in 1999.

She began riding motorcycles regularly in the early 1990's, and passionately determined to learn basic motorcycle mechanics so she could work on her own motorcycles. She has owned both Honda's and Harley Davidson motorcycles.

About 1998, the two women's riding clubs that Jasmine belonged to (Women in the Wind – Rocky Mountain Chapter and Freedom Chapter of Ladies of Harley) requested that she teach the ladies some wrenching tips. Jasmine's Motorcycle Maintenance Class for Women was born of these requests.

Jasmine has been teaching women (and a few men) how to do minor repairs and maintenance on their motorcycles since 1998. Most students report that they are much more comfortable with both their motorcycles and with talking to their mechanics after learning the basics about their motorcycles.

Jasmine hopes you will find the information in this book useful, even if you never turn a wrench yourself. Her hope is also that you will at a minimum, gain a better understanding of what is going on with your motorcycle.

Remember, this book provides only general guidelines. Also know that wrenching on your own machine carries its own responsibilities and liabilities.

Jasmine and Bluecreek Art Works and Motorcycle Training assume NO RESPONSIBILITY OR LIABILITY for work you may choose to do on your Motorcycle.

Jasmine wishes you many miles of SAFE Riding, Fun Roads and Happy Wrenching!

Also Available at: www.bluecreekartworks.com

Current MC Maintenance Articles you can check out

Maintenance Class Schedules (Denver area only)

Amateur MC Videos, including Deaf Rider Videos

Purchase or Read excerpts from Jasmine's First book:

Women In the Wind, Fearless Women of the 20th and 21st Centuries

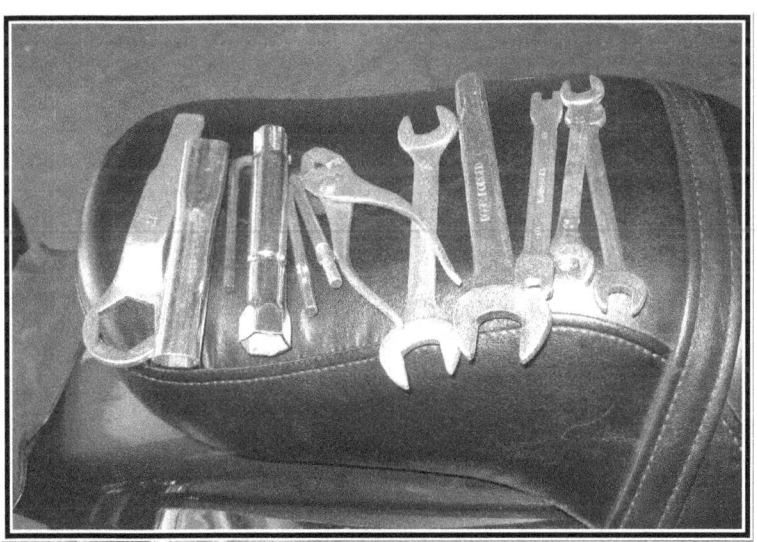

What are you waiting for? Get to IT!